Oh, the
MEETINGS
You'll
Go To!

Oh, the MEETINGS You'll Go To!

A Parody
by DR. SUITS

with illustrations by Zohar Lazar
creative direction by Christopher Sergio

PORTFOLIO
PENGUIN

I would like to dedicate this book to everyone who ever told me
I was the funniest person they know.
Instead I'm dedicating it to Asa, Charlotte, and Ivy,
who think those people are nuts.

Portfolio / Penguin
An imprint of Penguin Random House LLC
375 Hudson Street
New York, New York 10014

ISBN 9780735213982 (hardcover)

Printed in the United States of America
10 9 8 7 6 5 4 3 2 1

Creative direction by Christopher Sergio

Congratulations!
School's out, you're all done!
Now on to your dream job.
Get out there—have fun!

With your brand-new degree
and eager ambition,
you're destined for greatness,
and paid-off tuition!
You're all on your own now (five roommates aside),
and what you do next only **YOU** can decide.

With a latte in hand, you'll scan job sites for leads,
looking out for a job that will meet all your needs.
Go apply for them all, but hold out for big bucks;
you've got loans to pay off, and barista pay sucks.

And you'll get some rejections—
don't let them sink in;
go apply to ten more!
Go update your LinkedIn!

(Don't feel so hard up—
    or you'll join a doomed startup.)

But startups are trendy,
and loaded with perks.
They're casual and carefree,
and love all your quirks.

When your offer arrives
you'll be tickled to land
in a (low-paying) job
in an office open-planned.

OH!
THE MEETINGS YOU'LL GO TO!

You'll meet the world's brightest,
you'll hang with the best!
And now that you've met them,
you'll work with the rest.

You'll shimmer and shine as your confidence blooms.
You will rise through the ranks; you will rule conference rooms.
Whatever the task, you'll be faster than fast.
Your bosses will praise and promote you at last.

Except they won't yet.
First they want you to sweat.

Despite your clear brilliance,
you won't be the top.
And bleary
and weary,
you'll work till you drop.

You'll feel overworked.
(Can you die young from stress?)
Try not to melt down—
you're such a hot mess.

You'll sulk at your desk
and feed feelings with takeout,
play Adele on repeat,
your poor face will break out.

After late nights at work,
you will pass out, half-dead,
then find that it's hard
to get out of your bed.

Some meetings are loud and some induce groaning.
Sometimes you'll get tired of the PowerPoint droning.
If you want to contribute, you'll have to speak up.
Can you get a word in? Will they tell you to shut up?
You try, and your boss glares; you know that you've messed up.

I shouldn't have tried! I'm so stupid! I'm dumb!
you'll panic—but then you will see through the scrum
that your boss is now listening, she's paying attention!
What else should I say? What else should I mention?
Would mentioning "mobile" help break up the tension?

As you try to sound smart
your mind races ahead;
you recall with relief that smart tweet you just read:
This sounds like THAT thing that guy said at that TED.
But you've waited too long, and the meeting is dead.
No one's listening . . .

. . . because they're just waiting.
Waiting for the next day off,
for their pay to be raised, and their debts all paid off,
for the next compromise, and the next painful trade-off,
for the headhunter's call, or the news that they're laid off.
Or waiting around for a budget to spend,
or waiting around for this meeting to end.
Waiting, just waiting.

Waiting for Facebook to show something fun,
waiting for colleagues to get their work done,
waiting for growth, so the firm's number one;
for new standing desks to make their feet numb,
for surging to end so their Ubers can come.
Waiting, just waiting.

NO!
Don't let that be you!

Somehow you'll survive
all the doom and nay-saying.
You'll find the bright place
where T-Swift's always playing.

With tricks and with time,
you'll turn into a winner;
you'll advance, be a pro, not some wide-eyed beginner.
And soon you'll be treating your parents to dinner.

Oh, the meetings you'll go to! There's so much to fix!
Status updates at dawn, status check-ins at six.
Agendas to shorten, agendas to lengthen!
Budgets to cut and projections to strengthen.
You'll suck up to suckers, with nerds you'll be nerdy,
if your long game is good, you'll make partner by thirty.

But despite all your sweat,
You're still not there yet.

I'm afraid that you'll find
that the Boomers resent you.
They'll fear all your changes.
They'll stack cards against you.

Then it all falls apart.
Your work friends depart.
Your pet project fails—
you'll be back at the start.

And back at the start you'll feel lonely and small,
with no one to text and with no one to call.
You'll gripe and you'll moan, want to change your career.
You'll think you were foolish to want to be here.

But you'll have to press on.
Gotta pay back investors.
You'll have to press on.
Please the board of directors.

You'll have to press on.
Satisfy the inspectors.
Press on through the weekends, press on through the nights.
Though your coworkers leave you and turn out the lights.

On and on you will press;
you'll achieve Inbox Zero!
You'll talk on the *phone,*
you'll feel like a hero!

You'll burn out, of course.
You'll be pushing uphill.
Sometimes you'll just want
to Netflix and chill.
So sign up for Tinder,
chase after that thrill;
but chase it too far,
it will all go downhill.
The trick is to balance the work with the play.
Have fun!—but invest in your 401(k).

And will you survive?
Yes! You'll (probably) thrive!
It may take some time, but one day you'll arrive!

KID, YOU'LL BUILD EMPIRES!

So . . .
No matter your major or grades in the end,
or whether or not you make more than your friends,
you're off to great meetings,
so try to stay Zen!
Enjoy all the free coffee
    . . . *just have those copies by ten.*